Beach Boy

story and pictures by
Nicola Smee

COLLINS

First published 1987 by William Collins Sons & Co Ltd, London and Glasgow
© text and illustrations Nicola Smee 1987

The boy goes to the beach
early in the morning.

He loves the smell of the sea
and the sound of the waves
and the sand between his toes.

After a while he stops walking.
"This is the place for me," he says,
and takes a spade out of his box.

The boy works hard
and the warm dry sand
turns cold and wet
as he digs deeper.

The beach is filling up
with people now.
But the boy is too busy to notice.

At last his hole is deep enough, and . . .

. . . he digs a trench to the sea.

The sea trickles into his trench, then,
with the next big wave . . .

. . . the boy has his sea pool!

The children clap.

"Now for a swim," decides the boy.

He swims through the water like a fish.

The boy is hungry after his swim,
and he takes his lunch out of his box.

The boy is feeling tired.
He sits down and covers himself
with sand.

"Please will you cover my arms with sand," he asks Granny.

"Of course I will, dearie," says Granny.

Later on, Granny stops her knitting and takes a flask out of her basket.

"Would you care to join me in a cup of tea?"
she says.

"Just what I needed,"
smiles the boy.

As they pack up to go home,
Granny asks the boy, "May I wash
the sand off my feet in your pool?"
"Please do," he answers.

"How many grains of sand do
you think are on this beach?" asks the boy.

"Millions and millions," replies Granny.